The Storms and Tribulations of Marriage

JESUS ORDAINED MARRIAGE
JESUS' FIRST NON – HEALING MIRACLE
WAS A MARRIAGE

By

Dr. Willie Coburn

"Glory to God in the highest, and on earth, peace, goodwill toward men." Luke 2:14 NKJV

The Storms and Tribulations of Marriage

By:

Dr. Willie Coburn

Copyright@2015
All Rights Reserved
Printed in The United States of America

Published By:

ABM Publications
A division of Andrew Bills Ministries, Inc.
PO Box 6811, Orange, CA 92863
www.abmpublications.com

ISBN: 978-1-931820-51-6

All scripture quotations, unless otherwise indicated, are taken from The King James Version 1977, Thomas Nelson Publishing. It is used by permission, with all rights reserved.

TABLE OF CONTENTS

	Introduction	7
1	Communication	9
2	Prayer	13
3	Truth	17
4	Faith	21
5	Surrender	23
6	Financial	27
7	God's Yellow Pages	29
8	Scriptural Marriage Commands	31
9	Check Your Self	33
10	Walk With God	39
11	Neutral Party Counseling	45
12	Parent – Child Relationships	49
	About The Author	51

DR. WILLIE COBURN

ACKNOWLEDGMENTS

I am eternally gratefully to our Lord and Savior for the opportunity to complete this book.

I would like to give honor and thanks to my Christian Church Family, who suggested that I write this book.

To the Ministers who always say, "GOD IS GOOD ALL THE TIME AND ALL THE TIME GOD IS GOOD". Also, tell us what we need to know and not what we already know.

Special thanks to the late Rev. Dr. William R. Johnson, Jr. Presiding Elder, who encouraged me to continue my Christian Education studies.

I am forever grateful to the Minister Spouse's, Widows & Widowers Department for seeing in me what I didn't see in myself, in electing me for the President, Vice President, and Corresponding Secretary of the Minister's Spouses Department, in previous years.

My thanks to end- laws Eddie, Ruby, Johnnie the weightlifter, Cynthia, Linda, Terry, Lloyd, Pat, Curtis the photographer, Pete, children Natasha,

Monique, grandchildren; Quentin, Qyara, Jayden, other family members and friends.

Special thanks to my mother-in-law, Ms Vivian Brown the former 1st Black Queen of the Cotton Carnival Jubilee parade in Memphis Tennessee who made this previous marriage possible for me, to her daughter, Pastor Gloria Marshall - Virk, AKA "Pumpkin"

Finally, I would like to give thanks for everyone who came into my life to encourage me to continue the race.

INTRODUCTION

MINISTRY BEGINS AT HOME

Jesus said, "You shall love your neighbor as yourself." If you are married, your spouse is your closest neighbor!

When a man and a woman make the commitment to become husband and wife, there is often a joyous gathering to celebrate the establishment of a new family. A wedding is a joyous occasion, often accompanied with music, flowers, and friends. Marriage is one of the most important events in a person's life. A formal, public commitment begins a lifetime together, and the bride and groom may even say traditional words such as, "for better, for worse, for richer, for poorer, in sickness and in health, until death do us part."

The Bible states that marriage is a permanent relationship not to be divided (Mark 10:9). Marriage is instituted by God to accomplish His plans in our society. In marriage a husband and wife become "one" (Genesis 2:24), building a permanent relationship.

The phenomenon "that marriage is 50-50" is misleading. When husband and wife give 100 percent they have a strong relationship and the ability to deal with issues that will occur. Jesus said, "It is more blessed to give than to receive" (Acts 20:35).

No one needs to be mad at the other. Partner agrees or disagrees and takes the matter to the Lord. God can soften the heart of one or illuminate the heart of the other, but the Lord must be given prevalence in a stand still. Christ is the center of the relationship; trust Him to make it work. One of the most important assets in an effective ministry is a strong and healthy marriage. Many people in ministry are failing God because of problems in their homes that have been generated by their neglect. A neglect of the home is clear disobedience to God's standards for those who oversee his church.

The Bible tells us that an overseer must manage his own home well. In 1st Timothy 3:5, scripture tells us that "for if a man know not how to rule his own house, how shall he take care of the Church of God".

The ministry must first start within the home, within self, and then extend to others.

CHAPTER 1

COMMUNICATION

Communication is much more than words. It involves the entire personality.

Whether in marriage, selling a product or closing a deal, to be effective about anything takes knowledge, preparation and presentation along with the right attitude. The speaker needs to have his head and his heart both saying the same thing.

We communicate in a variety of ways in addition to using words. In fact, everything about us sends a message. Not only does the face communicate, but also the entire body and actions of a person.

Behavior and gestures can say different things at different times under different circumstances and in different places. In communication, how a person feels is always communicated, if not in words, then through his/her tone of voice or any of many nonverbal aspects.

Furthermore, communication is an exchange of thoughts and ideas between two partners. Communication is not about getting your point across. It's about hearing and understanding what the other person has to say.

Even though you may not agree with what is being said, you don't allow yourself to become angry or frustrated, because you know that in the initial stages of conversation, Clarity are the goal.

Ephesians 4:15, gives us a fundamental principle in communicating effectively "but, speaking the truth in love, may grow up in all things into Him who is the head – Christ."

Effective communication means effective listening as well as speaking. We should try to understand the other person's point of view, the others person's feelings and heeds.

When you talk with your husband or wife, do you demonstrate concern and care? Do you communicate with patience to each other?

1st Corinthians 13:4, "Love suffers long and is kind; does not envy; love does not parade itself, is not puffed up". Patience is a way of expressing love, as we see in 1st Corinthians 13, called the "love Chapter". We read, "love is patient; love is kind, love is not envious or boastful or arrogant or rude.

The success or failure of a marriage can depend on what happiness between a husband and wife during the day. Learn to express a positive, loving attitude when you are together. If you make this effort, you can avoid an accidental argument or an unnecessary grudge that will last and could lead to a divorce.

A positive word of encouragement or appreciation can make a big difference in your relationship. Christians who are maturing in Christ will care about how their words affect those who listen to them. Conflicts in marriage occurs when one spouse are not allowed to make their Contribution. Either one spouse speaks over the other striving to gain respect or one spouse speaks over the other refusing to give respect.

Our desire to be right or have it our own way pushes us to say more than we should. We have to be aware of the Devil and his schemes. One of his schemes is to have us say more than we should. According to Matthew 15:16, but those things which proceed out of the mouth come forth from the heart, and they defile the man.

DR. WILLIE COBURN

CHAPTER 2

PRAYER

The Bible says in Proverbs 3:5-6, "Trust in the Lord with all your heart, and Lean not on your own understanding; in all your ways acknowledge Him, and He shall direct your paths".

A marriage requires work, effort and continual nourishment to be successful. It means following all God –given responsibilities as a husband or as a wife. There will be obstacles, differences, and even conflicts. But with God's help, you can improve your marriage.

Seek God in any marriage conflicts; however, you cannot force your spouse to change – you can only change yourself. However, it is better to have prayer in the home, for a successful marriage than not having ongoing prayer as professing believing Christians.

Per Apostle Paul, "I can do all things through Christ who strengthens me".

When we pray seeking God's will first. He rearranges our priorities to match with His. God never tells us a method for answering our prayers, because often our prayers aren't in accordance with His will. Our goal when praying should always be to seek His will.

If our prayer request reflects His will, His answer will be yes, though not always in a form we expect. God cannot be put in a box. He doesn't always answer in the same ways.

Prayer is the nearest approach and the highest enjoyment of Him that we are capable of in our life.

Prayers Of the Heart:

Prayer should be the first thing we do in the morning and our focus should be on the Lord. Ps. 5:3, Mark 1:35

Pray for a peaceful and quiet life this is good and acceptable unto God. 1 Tim. 2:2 Pray a prayer of thanksgiving. Ps. 34:1-3, Ps. 103:1-5.

Pray to understand the mysteries of life God's way and not our way. Prov. 3:5-6, Is. 55:8-9.

Pray to live a victorious life where sin is not in control. Rom. 3:23, Rom. 6:23, 1st Cor. 15:56-57

Pray for God's wisdom to be manifested in the heart, mind and soul and that we worship the Lord in Spirit and Truth. Col. 1:19, John 4:24

Pray to be a zealous doer of God's Word. Titus 2:14

Pray for knowledge and kindness in the servants of God. Prov. 20:15, Eph. 4:32

Pray to hide God's Word in your heart so that sin will not dwell there. Ps. 119:11

Pray for the afflicted and needy to have justice. Ps. 82:3

We can think of prayer as a means of communicating with God. Prayer is a two way process. When we pray we should take time listening to God speaking to our hearts.

Sometimes we pray but never stop to hear what God has to say to us. So we miss our answers to our prayers.

Prayer is the most powerful force Christians have on this earth to help them other than the Power of the Holy Spirit.

Bible reading should be a great part of your life. God speaks to man through His word. The Bible tells us the Word was made flesh and dwelt among us (John 1:14); the Word washes (St John 15:13); the Word is Truth (St. John 17:17); the Word is living and powerful and sharper than any two-edge sword (Hebrews 4:12). Therefore, to have a powerful prayer life we must study the Bible as well as pray.

For the Bible teaches "My people are destroyed for lack of knowledge (Hosea 4:6). If we want knowledge of God and Power in our lives, we should study the word of God and live a prayerful life.

God answers every question we need to know, through His Word or prayer. We all need to acknowledge God and our savior in every aspect of our lives.

CHAPTER 3

TRUTH

Proverbs 3:3, states "Let not mercy and truth forsake you; bind them around your neck, write them on the tablet of your heart'. Also, Ephesians 4:13, says till we all come to the unity of faith and of the knowledge of the Son of God, to a perfect man, to the measure of the statue of the fullness of Christ.

Marriage is the most intimate relationship two human beings can experience, second only to a relationship with God.

Seeking counsel from a pastor or from the Elders of the church should not Create a life time of hospitality toward the spouse. Getting counseling is an excellent way to clear misconceptions about marriage roles, to see a situation from another viewpoint, and to distinguish between God's standards and those of the world.

Ephesians 5:21:33, gives specific instructions for how both husbands and wives ought to act towards one another. "A husband is to love his wife as Christ loves the church and gave Himself for her" verse 25. The concept that marriage is a 50-50 decision is misleading. When both people give 100 percent, you have a strong relationship and the ability to cope with crises and problems.

When one spouse is demonstrating 100 percent control in the marriage, this will lead to crises and problems in the relationship. When a husband is committed to demonstrating love for his wife, and wife is committed to graciously allowing her husband to lead, the marriage will work.

Acts 20:35, states "it more blessed to give than to receive", which is foundational to a happy relationship for eternal life,

Communicating truth in love is the key to being heard because only when we communicate to others their value in our eyes will they be able to accept hard truths Ephesians 4:15. Speaking the truth in love is absolutely essential for conflict resolution and this is particularly true in marriage. God said blessed are the peacemakers, and that is always the goal for Christians. Matthew 5:9.

You shall know the truth and the truth shall set you free. We need to stand free and to know what true freedom is. Life is full of many choices and there is a sure path (Jeremiah 6:16), we can take. We all have to make decisions in various areas of life on a daily basis.

The truth about something that is relative to just one situation and then changes to fit another situation. Truth is constant, never changing. Having a working knowledge of what truth really is and how to walk in the truth will help you to make the right decisions in your life. There is only one truth.

God's word to us declares that God's light and in Him is no darkness. When a person has the truth opened up to them, then they can see the truth has been revealed. True revelation can only come through those who have a relationship with God through Jesus Christ.

DR. WILLIE COBURN

CHAPTER 4

FAITH

Hebrews 11:1, states "now faith is the substance of things hoped for, the evidence of things not seen". Also, Hebrew 11:6, but without faith it is impossible to please Him, for he who comes to God must believe that He is, and that He is a rewarded of those who diligently seek Him".

Ephesians 2:8-9, makes it clear, for by grace you have been saved through faith and that not of yourselves, it is the gift of God,, also, not of works, lest anyone should boast. It is not obtained by our power. It is simply given to us by God, along with His grace and mercy, according to His holy plan and purpose, and because of that. He gets all the glory

In Luke 7:50, Jesus said to the woman, "your faith has saved you. Go in peace". The woman believed in Jesus by faith and faith is what sustains us to the end.

First Peter 1:8-9, Whom having not seen you love. Though now you do not see Him, yet believing, you rejoice with joy inexpressible and full of glory.

Receiving the end of your faith-the salvation of your souls.

Faith is essential in a relationship. Without demonstrating faith and trust in God, we have no place with Him. James 1:2-4, tells us "my brethren, count it all joy when you fall into various trials and knowing that the testing of your faith produces patience. Also, but let patience have its perfect work, that you may be perfect and complete, lacking nothing ."

Our faith can stumble at times, but because it is the gift of God, given to His children. Jesus provides times of trial and testing in order to prove that our faith is real and to sharpen and strengthen it.

CHAPTER 5

SURRENDER

When two people are united in Christ, their goal is to grow in Christ likeness throughout the life of the marriage. When both partners make becoming more like Christ their individual goal is strong. A Christian marriage begins with the understanding that the Bible gives a clear description of the roles of husband and wife found in Ephesians 5 and commitment to fulfilling those roles.

Wives are to submit to their husbands "as to the Lord, Ephesians 5:22", not because they are to be subservient to them, but because both husbands and wives are to "submit to one another out of reverence for Christ "Ephesians 5:33, and because there is to be an authority structure within the home, with Christ at the head, Ephesians 5:23-24.

Mutual love, respect and submission are the cornerstone of a Christian marriage.

When God brought Eve to Adam in the first marriage, she was made from his "flesh and bone" Genesis 2:21 and they became "one flesh."

Genesis 2:23-24. Becoming one flesh means more than just a physical union. It means a meeting of the mind and soul to form one unit.

One's vertical relationship with God goes a long way toward ensuring that the horizontal relationship between a husband and wife is a lasting, and therefore God-honoring.

Strong Christian marriages are characterized by the spiritual disciplines, Bible study, Scripture memory, prayer, and meditation on the things of God. When both partners practice these disciplines, each is strengthened and matured, which naturally strengthens and matures the marriage. When we bring a "sacrifice of praise," we choose to believe that, even though life is not going as we think it should. God is still good and can be trusted. Nahum 1:7.

When we choose to praise God in spite of the storms, Jesus is honored, and our faith grows deeper Malachi 3:13-17.

God comforts us in all our troubles, so that we can comfort those in any trouble with the comfort we ourselves have received from God. 2 Corinthians 1:4.

Furthermore, the Bible teaches "do not let any unwholesome talk come out of your mouths, but only what is helpful for building others up according to their needs, that it may benefit those who listen." Ephesians 4:29

DR. WILLIE COBURN

CHAPTER 6

FINANCIAL

When we find ourselves facing trials, the first place we should go for help is God.

King David, a man after God's own heart, learned to look to God and depend on Him more than man. The book of Hebrews encourages us to come boldly to God. Even though we can feel beaten down by financial trials.

Scriptures tells us in 1st Peter 5:7, "casting all your care upon Him, for He cares for you". God is concerned about all of us. He wants each of us to have an abundant life and enjoy our work. Since God cares for us, we should turn to Him to help us in our time of need.

The Bible gives a clear description of the roles of husband and wife in a Christian marriage: Matthew 19:6, Jesus states, "What God has joined together let no man separate".

Romans 7:2, "for the woman who has a husband is bound by the law to her husband as long as he lives".

Malachi 2:16, "for the Lord God of Israel says that He hates divorce.

1st Corinthians 7:10-24, "a wife is not to depart from her husband, "and verse 11 adds that a husband is not to divorce his wife.

The Bible gives two clear grounds for divorce: (1) sexual immorality (Matthew 5:32, 19:9), and (2) abandonment by an unbeliever (1st Corinthians 7:15).

According to the Bible, divorce for the following reasons is not justifiable, financial reasons, employer business closed, loss of unemployment, reduction in income, laid off, home foreclosure, or medical conditions.

1st Corinthians 4:6, explains none of these can be claimed to be biblical grounds for a divorce. However, our first steps should be confession, forgiveness, reconciliation, and restoration. To put in postmodern terms, face the difficulties and work out the differences.

CHAPTER 7

GOD'S YELLOW PAGES

Let your fingers do the walking through the Bible

Mark 9:50 – Have peace with one another

James 5:16 – Pray for one another

Galatians 5:13 - Serve one another

Ephesians 4:12 - Be kind and forgiving to one another

John 13:34 – Love one another

Romans 14:19 – Build up one another

Romans 12:6 – Be of the same mind toward one another

Romans 15:7 – Receive one another

Romans 12:10 – Submit to one another

1st Thessalonians – 12:10 – Comfort one another

1st Peter 3:8 – Be compassionate with one another

James 5:16 – Confess your faults to one another

Romans 14:1 – Accept one another

To solve marriage storms, **we must not:**

Galatians 5:15 - Use each other

Romans 14:1 - Judge one another

1st Corinthians 6:1-7 – Take one another to court

Titus 3:3 – Hate one another

Galatians 5:26 – Provoke or envy one another

Colossians 3:9 – Lie to one another

CHAPTER 8

SCRIPTURAL MARRIAGE COMMANDS

Pray together daily: Psalm 127:1, Unless the Lord builds the house, they labor in vain who build it. Unless the Lord guards the city. The watchman stays awake in vain.

Talk together regularly: Proverbs 27:6, He who sends a message by a fool, cuts off his own feet and drinks violence.

Proverbs 26:25, When he speaks kindly , do not believe him, for there are even abominations in his heart.

Throw yourself into your relationship: Colossians 3:23, Whatever you do, work at it with all your heart, as working for the Lord, not for men.

Forgive your spouse: Colossians 3:13, Bear with each other and forgive whatever grievances you may have against one another, Forgive as the Lord forgave you.

Serve your spouse: Galatians 5:13, Serve one another in love.

Speak lovingly and respectfully: Proverbs 25:11, A word aptly spoken is like apples of gold in settings of silver.

CHAPTER 9

CHECK YOUR SELF

Some people love mayhem, dysfunction, and disorder. God has a purpose for everything. There are things that can easily distract you from your destination. It seems when you are almost at your destination, an unseen event /mishap occurs which leads to a delay in your progress. When there is confusion one has to look at what is going on and what can they learn from the situation. There are always solutions to problems. It's a matter of how you view and solve it with Gods guidance. God is not the author of confusion, but of peace, 1st Corinthians 14:33.

When a home is not covered with prayer, peace, unity, joy, and love, with no mutual boundaries agreed upon, that creates havoc in the home. Unity is an issue when one person wants to do their own thing and ignore the other person's feelings. Respect and a lack of compassion is lacking in that individual. No one should get hostile or aggressive over minute things.

When the same vision is not agreed upon which will lead to a divide and conquer in the household? Hostility, anger and threats will invade a home if the lines of positive communication aren't being exemplified between each other. Therefore, guidance can be manifested in Galatians 5:22-23 and Proverbs 14:1.

When you talk "to" each other rather than talking "at" each other. Communication and boundaries should be established before a conversation is pursued. When someone is angry they should cool off first before they begin a conversation. This will reduce stress and havoc in the atmosphere. This will lead to a more intense and in depth conversation when everyone is alert and calm.

Putting someone else's feelings ahead of yours will show humility and compassion. Try not to exert your authority and demands on the other person. Admit your wrongs because the other person doesn't want to hear your excuses. Open door policy between each other will strengthen any relationship. When someone is yelling, and shouting at the other person, that person is being demeaned/subhuman.

Do not throw a tantrum or freeze your spouse out. Be respectful and be a good listener. Acknowledge what the other person is saying and how that makes them feel.

Resist making promises or agreement with friends before confirming with spouse. Boundaries should be established before you make any form of commitments to anyone.

Talking to your spouse about commitments or engagements with friends is necessary so that there will not be any miscommunication or lack of knowledge of the situation. No one wants to hear gossip through the rumor mill about their spouse. Trying to resolve sticky dilemmas aren't fun especially when it could have been avoided in the beginning by having an honest conversation with your spouse.

Don't entertain friends who are negative about your spouse. According to Prov. 16:28. A perverse man sows strife, and a whisperer separates the best of friends. The friends don't contribute any positive energy or healthy vibes to endure and sustain a relationship. If you start listening to their negativity then you will begin to start feeling the same way towards your spouse. You will start to have some doubt about that person's capabilities and character.

If they don't have anything positive to contribute then you should ignore them and their destructive comments. Sometimes others can see something in a person that you cannot see and it may be important which can be a signal that there are some hidden destructive flaws that can't be overcome.

Satan is busy creating conflicts in the family and relationships. Studies have shown during the course of marriage there are external and internal power and control struggles over one spouse leadership and recognition in the home. The spouse doesn't want to compromise nor give up their authority. Humbleness is not in the spouse's vocabulary. No compassion or empathy for anyone. Furthermore, there is neither respect nor consideration for the other person's feelings.

There should be some form of compromising on both sides. No one should dominate another person. Why should one person give away all of their self-control and self-respect to appease another?

Each person should bring their personal strengths to the relationship and look at their weakness not as failure but how to improve in that area. You should not be putting yourself on a pedestal and the other person is a sub servant position. Sometimes it is difficult for that person to see your side of the equation until it happens to them.

Spouses with jobs and ministry must take time for leisure to avoid having and negative effect on their marriage. Spouses must prioritize their work first before their marriage and family. Even when they are with their family they are absent minded and not present because they are thinking about other things.

This puts a strain on the marriage because one spouse is actually being ignored and their desires aren't being met. No quality time is being spent with the spouse or family due to either workaholic or they just don't respect their spouse and with selfish ego's and no boundaries established.

Due to one person controlling the marriage relationship, and not following God's laws in the relationship. This will lead to a dissolve and demise of the relationship. Without proper communication, Satan will come in and demised God's covenant. Relationships are built on communication, trust, boundaries, gifts of the Spirit, (Galatians 5:22-23) and compassion. Without the gifts of the Spirit these, demonic forces will seek and wreak havoc in a marriage.

DR. WILLIE COBURN

CHAPTER 10

WALK WITH GOD

A personal walk with God comes to us through wisdom and revelation. We turn to God and He renews our Strength so that we can run and not grow weary, so that we can walk and not feel faint.

The man or woman who turns to God is like a tree planted by a stream. We must walk with God, seek wisdom and revelation. Also, we should find people who walked with God to walk with us through our life.

A growing love relationship with God is permanent to everything else that happens in the Christian life. That's why we were created, that's why Jesus died on the cross for our sins and that's why God is preparing an eternal home for us in heaven. Our relationship with God is a personal relationship.

We should not let anyone or anything comes between us and God. If we are not grounded in God's Word, and we do not know the voice of the

Holy Spirit in us, and then we are vulnerable to bad advice or even false doctrine.

We must ask ourselves is it possible to intimately know the God of the universe?

We must fellowship with Him moment by moment. There will be storms and conflicts beyond our control. At times, our peace must come from God's word. Only the power of God enables us to keep our character intact. We must lean into God's grace, love and power. And we must pray.

Our best connection to God's power is on our knees in sweet conversation with Him. He is our source, our righteousness, our character in all. Without Him, we can hang up our gloves because the fight is over. Walking with God leads to receiving his intimate counsel, and counseling leads to deep restoration. As we learn to walk with God and hear his voice, he is able to bring up issues in our hearts that need speaking to.

In the presence of God, and removed from distractions, we are able to hear him more clearly, and a secure environment has been established for the broken places in our hearts.

Research have shown that partners whose marriage lasted over 20 years found that faith Communication, and prayer overcame spiritual warfare in their marriage. Spiritual warfare is resisting, overcoming and defeating the enemy's lies that he sends our way.

Spiritual warfare is dealing with three key things the enemy sends at us: temptations, deception and accusations. Spiritual warfare comes in two ways: offensive and defensive. Offensive warfare is tearing down the strongholds the enemy has formed in our mind through deception and accusations, and defensive warfare is guarding our self against the tactics or schemes of the devil.

Since strongholds are built upon lies that we have been fed, the way we tear down strongholds is by feeding on the truth (in God's Word), which is the opposite of what the enemy has been feeding us.

Today, we need to take up the sword of the Spirit (God's Word), and start slaughtering the enemy's assets that he's been using against us. Partners must learn to walk with God together, pray for each other and cover each other's back.

You cannot let the threats of the enemy grow in your mind.. You must cast down those thoughts

as they come, putting them in their rightful place. "Neither give place to the devil", Ephesians 4:27.

The spirits of Jezebel will:

--seek to get you out of the race; do not want that person part of the circle or congregation.

--seek to run you out of town
--seek to influence those in power to listen and do evil to people

--Jezebel wants you to run from threats
--Jezebel wants to intimidate the children of God
--Jezebel will try to get you sidetracked
--Jezebel is a lying spirit and an accusing spirit

--The Jezebel spirit always wants to be looked at as the light of the world and all bowed down in the presence of Jezebel

The Jezebel spirit often operates through prophetic people – either by direct action, or by discouragement. The spirit of Jezebel will stop the remodeling of God's house being done in a professional like manner, due to misgivings, or start things that won't be completed.

The spirit mind of Jezebel will advise a person not to attend an institution that does not look favorably on gender. One should persevere without having huge consequences. People must go through God's steps because if not when they do get promoted, it won't last. There are great people in the Bible that have done outstanding achievements. When there's conflict it won't stay for long. Respect and prayer plays a big role in our postmodern society.

Today, we need to take up the sword of the Spirit (God's Word), and start slaughtering the enemy's assets that he's been using against us.

Partners must learn to walk with God together, pray for each other and cover each other's back.

DR. WILLIE COBURN

CHAPTER 11

NEUTRAL PARTY COUNSELING

Sometimes when a couple can't rectify their marriage situation, then sometimes it's best to seek help from God first then a neutral third party. Couples should ride it out first by trying to resolve their own issues. Every time you have a problem you need to pray with your spouse not with your friend.

Women tend to seek advice from their friends first before seeking God. When you invite and confide in your friends you are breaking down the dynamics of the relationship.

When you ask help from others, some people want to solve their problems. Both parties must own up to their part in the breakdown of communication in the relationship. Seeking counseling sometimes can be a relief for both parties.

The following are biblical scriptures for solving marriage conflicts:

Matthew 7:12—Therefore all things whatsoever ye would that men should do to you, do ye even so to them.

Ephesians 4:32—And be kind one to another, tenderhearted, forgiving one another even as God for Christ's sake hath forgiven you.

Galatians 6:2—Bear ye one another's burdens, and so fulfill the law of Christ. Many times people fail to reveal their needs to members of their own family and embarrassed to let others know about family issues.

Galatians 2:11—But when Peter was come to Antioch, I withstood him to the face, because he was to be blamed. Face to face communication in self-control will help in many family relationships

James 5:16—Confess your faults one to another, and pray one for another, that ye may be healed. The effectual fervent prayer of a righteous man availeth much.

Matthew 18:15, 16, 17,—If your brother sins against you, first discuss it privately with him. But if this does not resolve it, get help. Take one of two other Christians with you. Then the Bible says to take the matter before the congregation.

If even this does not solve the conflict, then the one is clearly in sin must be withdrawn from. 2 Thess. 3:15.

Getting counseling is an excellent way to clear misconceptions about marriage roles, to see a situation from another viewpoint, and to distinguish between God's master plan for marriage and the world concept.

The scriptures provide us to all good works, including how to solve problems in our homes. We can solve our problems God's way. If we do not do so; we have no one to blame but ourselves.

Seek out professional marriage advice, even if your spouse will not seek counseling, you should go.

DR. WILLIE COBURN

CHAPTER 12

PARENT - CHILD RELATIONSHIPS

Parents should not be their child's friend because it blurs the line. Children need discipline, structure, and guidance. Some children as they get older love to put parents against each other, hoping that they get their way. This is disruptive and aggressive behavior. Therefore, parents should establish boundaries for their children.

Both parents should be in agreement as to how they will handle discipline. Children tell tales to get their parents to fight their wicked battles for them especially when they aren't doing well in school. They sometimes manipulate half-truths to deflect the attention on them. In a home all children should embrace respect, affliction, responsibility, love compassion, and honesty,

During our life time, all of us will experience storms; it is how we handle the issue, what is important. These storms are called divorce, loss of a child, loss of home, betrayal, ill health, abuse, loss of employment, death, all kinds of addiction.

But the Christian can find help in Scripture, through what the word of God says:

--Romans 8:28, "We know that God causes all things to work together for good to those who love God, to those who are called according to His purpose".

--Psalm 145:18, "The Lord is near to all who call upon Him, to all who call upon Him in truth".

--Matthew 7:8, "Everyone who asks receives, and he who seeks finds, and to him who knocks it will be opened".

--Matthew 21:22, All things you ask in prayer, believing, you will receive".

--Mark 6:47-48, Jesus was with each person in the storm, He did not leave them alone, Jesus is always with us.

God's promises, He will always be the same-never wavering.

ABOUT THE AUTHOR

As stated in the Scripture, "Trust in the Lord with all your heart, lean not on your understanding; in all your ways acknowledge Him, and He shall direct your paths." Proverbs 3:5-6

As the Apostle Paul wrote, "I can do all things through Christ who strengthens me." Philippians 4:13

Willie Coburn was born in Mississippi. At a young age, he accepted Christ as Lord and Savior and joined Jerusalem Temple Pentecostal Church in Mississippi.

After graduating from the public school system of Mississippi, he then attended Alcorn University studying Business Administration

He served six years in the United States Army as an accounting specialist during the Vietnam era and was honorably discharged.

In 1987, he was 1 of 9 individuals who started Showers of Blessing Missionary Baptist Church in Hesperia, California, which is very active today. He also, started a Gospel Quartet Group known as the Heavenly Stars, who performed throughout Southern California and Las Vegas for many years.

Years later, he married Pastor Gloria Marshall Virk, and then he began an Evangelism Ministry, as 1st Man, working in local church and held numerous positions in local church and in the Ministers' Spouses, Widows/ Widowers Dept. He was also, was elected as the 1st male spouse to serve as president of the Los Angeles/San Diego District Ministers' Spouse Widows/Widowers Dept.

He retired from the banking industry of 23 years, where he held numerous management positions. However, as a Real Estate Broker, he considered this his part-time hobby, while spending time with his grandkids.

Dr. Willie Coburn teaches Theology at a local Bible College and also conducts career development, financial, and ministry workshops and seminars throughout various cities.

CONTACT INFORMATION

The Storms and Tribulations of Marriage

All Books by Dr. Willie Coburn can be found for sale online in most major retailer sites or Christian Book Stores as softcover printed books or Ebooks.

For more information, you may contact us at:

Website:
glrsilverlakes.com

Email:
willieglr00@gmail.com

Or If you desire to order by mail, then please send your check or money order, with the attached form to:

Dr. Willie Coburn
PO Box 1142
Victorville, California 92393

DR. WILLIE COBURN

Print
Name_____

_____

Address_____

_____
_____

City_____

State_____**Zip**_____

Phone_____

When ordering by mail,
please allow 15-20 days for delivery

THANK YOU

www.ingramcontent.com/pod-product-compliance
Lightning Source LLC
Chambersburg PA
CBHW060858050426
42453CB00008B/1015